About This Book

Hey, it's Titus! If you are an entrepreneur or someone that is wanting to get into entrepreneurship, in this book you will find my experience on how I have got to where I am today and the things I have encountered leading up to the place of walking away from my job and jumping into the business world.

Business is a learned process. We learn something new each day. Success isn't instant and I've also learned that you can grow a small business out of business just as fast as you get it started, so this is just a starter manual to get things off the ground and what's on my heart.

MY STORY

As you start reading this book, I want you to put yourself in my shoes as an entrepreneur. I'm Titus Curry and I'll be telling you my story of entrepreneurship. In my opinion entrepreneurship is an unexpected and expected journey. You don't know what to expect but you have expectations of what you want.

You may not know, but I'm an owner of a detailing business and retail store of detailing products. This book is being produced when I'm 25 years old. I started my business after high school, doing family members mostly and started doing some friends and outsiders later. Don't get bored with me, but I was charging $25 to $50 per vehicle and working my sister and her boyfriend then and her husband now. We were doing about 4 vehicles per weekends sometimes more if none of them didn't cancel on us, which would always be a heartbreak!

After high school I worked for a lumber company for a while and when I was there, I would get appointments, but I would only take them for the weekends because I worked Monday through Friday. Each weekend I would be so happy to schedule those appointments. It helped me realize that I could grow something. It was always a high feeling to get a call about a job and they would make the appointment with me. But guess what? I wasn't making any money! I would pay my sister and brother-in-law their money and be left with like $75 to $100, only to turn around and reinvest in products.

I didn't know how to calculate cost for products and labor when quoting jobs. I would just charge based on hopefully they would take the price and be happy enough to book with me. I was booked every weekend and hardly ever made money to be profitable.

Well, as I kept doing that, I became more popular with others for detailing. My boss at the time started asking me how many I had to do for the weekend, and I would have like 5 or 6 on schedule. Now mind you, these were basic washes and basic interior cleans. We didn't do a lot of shampooing or waxing, maybe a little and I still didn't know how to properly charge for that.

We did that for a while, and I kept learning to advertise my brand and it grew just as I thought it would. I begin to become more booked with appointments. I started booking appointments on weekdays but after my job hours I kept showing my brand to others. I would get off at maybe 4pm and do one car and that's when I started doing the deeper things of detailing, and becoming more attentive to what I was doing. WE HAD A PRICE RISE! Pricing is something most entrepreneurs will deal with when getting into business. Playing it safe with pricing, and not being confident will cause you to miss out on a lot of compensation opportunities. That was a BIG problem for me as I grew and became more valuable.

As I'm doing this business on the side of my job, I begin to become more entrepreneurial and changing my mind on things. I begin to see how my job operated versus working for myself. I started losing interest in my job. When I first got started at the lumber company, I was excited and happy to have a job. I got paid $9 per hour operating a forklift, which was CRAZY!

But yes, I started changing my mind on working for myself and I started slacking on my job. Now that could be a bad thing for some people. My job became a hinder to my business. Personally, I tried to do the two together, but that didn't work. Some say to make you job your first investor but that's not always the best advice. Sometimes you have to just jump out there with nothing and make things happen. I originally was supposed to stay at work until 4pm but I wanted to leave at 2pm to do at least one car before the day. Sometimes you must just take a leap of faith and go for what you believe in. Life doesn't wait on no one and the time is now. With the way this world is going you can't take the risk of not taking risks and then living in fear and regret.

So, with that being said I took a couple of days off to get away from my job and maybe do some detailing and that second day I told my wife I didn't want to go back. Just with that support right there, I had no one else in my way because when she had my back, I was GOOD! That's a lesson to be learned, when you want to do anything in life the people around you should always support you. Failure is the best experience and teacher. My wife had confidence in me that I would provide and be there for her as the man of the house. She didn't know if I would succeed at my vision. We had just got married and moved into our new place and here I am talking about I wanted to quit my job. I also had told her to quit her job, so she was at home with a husband full of potential. She didn't pressure me with her wants in life and I'm grateful for that. She never gave me a hard time. That played a big part in growing my business. She had every right to express her wants and desires because as stated before, I told her to stay home and don't work. As I had the potential to grow my business and be successful. I could have easily FAILED.

Just like my wife was there for me, make sure the people around you can pour into you the wisdom and encouragement you need to get your vision going and keep it going. Entrepreneurship takes a strong mind because it's a process. Instant gratification is what everyone wants but that's not reality. Reality is you have to build and stay consistent. Keep your brand in front of your potential clientele.

Even as a new entrepreneur of detailing, I struggled with business. I wasn't able to just dive into detailing completely. I tried several ventures like selling insurance, being a medical courier, being a notary and signing agent. There were times I didn't detail but 2 or 3 vehicles per week and that wasn't sustainable for my home income. But God always provided for me with work in my other skill sets while building my detailing business. This process let me know that without sacrifice you can't expect to get what you want because if it was that easy, we'd all have what we want.

That's why you have the 1% mindset and the 99% mindset! The 1% lives on purpose the 99% doesn't. There is so much more to that but life still has much more to teach us. My story doesn't stop there. Today we are still running and doing great in business because of consistency. Consistency goes a long way in business. It's what compensates you in the long run. We do ceramic coatings, paint corrections, full details, interior and exterior and adding more services as we train and grow. YOUR STORY could be mine in some way, so I'd say KEEP BUILDING!

BE DECISIVE

As an entrepreneur you may ask what is being decisive? Decisiveness is very essential in your entrepreneur journey. You must make decisions for yourself, your business, and your family with the right balance. You don't want to waste time making decisions because it can put you behind. As an entrepreneur you want to stay ahead of your competitors and on top of marketing strategies. From my personally experience, I had to learn this for myself and I'm still learning. The key is that you don't have to be a 10 to teach a 3, all you must be is a 4.

Through your entrepreneurship you will see that people will try to dictate to your decisions and that can be hard sometimes to take judgment or criticism from outsiders. That's not always bad though. You must make investment decisions as an entrepreneur and take sound advice but, in the end, you are going to have to make the decision because you are the BOSS!

Make the decision every day to DECIDE! Personally, I have learned that to grow my business I need to be decisive. Indecisiveness can cause procrastination and procrastination will cause you to go out of business. You can't do business by yourself in a sense of scaling it. My goal is to grow my brand into a multi-million-dollar brand from Alabama and that definitely won't be just detailing all types of vehicles, but even in that I know that it will not work if I don't decide to make changes and get out of my selfish ways. Selfish as in thinking I can only do detailing by myself or I can run my store myself without paying someone to run it and even doing HR work behind the scenes myself. YOU CAN NOT DO IT ALONE! This is a decision you and I will have to make because as a detailer the first thing I think is I can make the money for myself and don't need help. You must consider that with help we could make more and expand my territory. The biggest companies in the world today are merging to take over. We as detailers and business owners must learn that working together and networking can only help us grow and evolve. You may even have to work with someone that you may not totally agree with in business. But in business its not personal it's business.

A lot of people say they are going to be financially free, have a successful million-dollar business, buy their time back and that's all good but affirmations without actions will equal nothing but selfish gain and lies to yourself and your future. Have you ever heard that talk is cheap? Some important characteristics of success to me is solving problems, impacting others, and bringing others together. BE DECISIVE for you not them!

ADD VALUE

Detailing is very much essential in the world today but in my opinion; people could detail their own vehicles. But, they won't! Why? Because life is busy and people don't find that it's a priority most times to clean their vehicle. Detailers must add more value than a drive thru car wash. Your client wants the best detail you can give them and it's your job to draw them back to you. Over delivering is always a great initiative. If your customers get the lowest of all your packages, it's a must that you provide value where they think not but can still be realized.

Building a genuine relationship with your customer can take you a long way in business. Transaction to transaction can always end because there is no reason for the customer to hold on to you and get another detailer that does just as good as you. So, build that close relationship. You can still operate professionally and have a relationship with your customers. The relationship doesn't mean that they can take advantage of you. Some believe that since you have a good business relationship, they can play on you for discounts and special deals. Never lower you value because its hard to get that back. The next time will be expected the same thing.

There are a lot of detailers out there, ask yourself what makes you different? What value can you bring to your customers that makes you their number one choice? Even if you are not in the detailing industry, ask yourself the same questions. What separates you from your competitor?

Your industry needs you and you must sometimes take that door and kick it down, rather than be asked to come in because some people don't want you in there anyway. Show up with your value and take the access! Your value is you that no one else has. Be the person everyone is looking for! As a growing detailer or even new business owner, its good to train and learn new services and provide that extra value to your customers but don't feel down when you can't go to different events and classes to learn new skills and get that extra information. We have to learn to crawl, walk, then run. In my industry some people connect with you because you are growing and they see the Facebook posts, just to send you a class that they are putting on and that's good. You should learn more and grow, but a relationship shouldn't be built only on if you come to my class and learn how to build you business and learn a new skill. Always help the next upcoming the best you can without putting them down and bashing them. As a new detailer know who is for you and who isn't. You too ENTREPRENEUR!

CUSTOMER SERVICE

WHAT CAUSES CUSTOMERS TO COME BACK?

There are several factors that can cause customers to become repeat customers.

Quality of service: Customers are more likely to become repeat customers if they receive high-quality service. This includes both the quality of the work performed and the customer service experience. If you consistently provide excellent service, customers are more likely to return to your business.

Consistency: Consistency is key in retaining repeat customers. If you consistently provide high-quality service, customers are more likely to trust you and return to your business. Inconsistent service, on the other hand, can lead to customers seeking out other options.

Personalization: Customers appreciate personalized service. If you take the time to get to know your customers and their needs, you can tailor your service to meet their specific needs. This can make customers feel valued and appreciated, which can lead to repeat business.

Communication: Communication is important in building relationships with customers. If you communicate clearly and promptly with customers, they are more likely to trust you and return to your business.

Incentives: Offering incentives, such as loyalty programs, discounts, and referral rewards, can encourage customers to return to your business. If customers feel they are getting a good value for their money, they are more likely to become repeat customers.

Trust: Trust is a key factor in retaining repeat customers. If customers trust you and your business, they are more likely to return to your business. This trust can be built through consistent high-quality service, personalized service, and good communication.

Overall, repeat customers are more likely to return to a business that provides high-quality, consistent service, personalized attention, clear communication, incentives, and builds trust with its customers.

WHY IS CAR DETAILING IMPORTANT?

Maintaining the appearance of your car: Regular detailing helps keep your car looking its best. It removes dirt, grime, and other contaminants that can accumulate on your car's exterior, making it look dull and unappealing.

Protecting your car's paint: Detailing helps protect your car's paint from the elements. A good wax or sealant helps prevent damage from UV rays, dirt, and other contaminants, and helps preserve the shine and color of your car's paint. Today we have the ceramic coatings, where you don't have to no longer necessarily wax your vehicle on a monthly or quarterly basis. Coatings have a longer duration and let's not forget (PPF) Paint Protection Film which gives an impact protection from rock chips for instance and preserves the paint with more mils of protection.

Preserving your car's value: Regular detailing can help preserve the resale value of your car. A well-maintained car with a clean and shiny exterior and interior is more attractive to potential buyers and can command a higher price.

Promoting a healthy driving environment: Interior detailing helps remove dirt, dust, and other allergens from your car's interior, promoting a healthy driving environment. It also helps remove unpleasant odors and can make your car's interior smell fresh and clean.

Identifying potential problems: Detailing provides an opportunity to inspect your car closely for any signs of damage or wear and tear. This can help you catch potential problems early on and address them before they become more serious and expensive to fix.

Overall, car detailing is important for both the aesthetic and functional aspects of your car, and can help keep your car looking and running its best for years to come.

Marketing For Everyone

Here are some marketing tips for detailing that can help you attract and retain customers.

Establish an online presence, Create a website and social media accounts for your detailing business or business. Use them to showcase your work, post before-and-after photos, and engage with potential and existing customers.

Offer a range of services and consider offering a variety of detailing services, from basic washes to full interior to exterior details to paint correction to ceramic coatings and more. This will attract a wider range of customers and increase your revenue potential.

Provide excellent customer service and make sure your customers are happy with the service you provide. Listen to their concerns and feedback, and be responsive to their needs.

Offer loyalty programs and incentives to reward your regular customers with loyalty programs, discounts, and other incentives. This will encourage them to return to your business and recommend you to others.

Network with other businesses and partner with other businesses in your community, such as auto repair shops, car dealerships, and car rental companies. Offer them discounts on your services in exchange for referrals.

Use targeted advertising and consider advertising on local websites, directories, and publications. You can also use targeted online ads to reach potential customers in your area.

Attend car shows and events, attend local car shows and events to showcase your work and promote your business. You can also offer on-site detailing services at these events.

Stay up-to-date with industry trend and keep up with the latest detailing techniques, products, and equipment. This will help you offer the best possible service to your customers and stay ahead of your competitors.

By implementing these marketing tips, you can increase your visibility and attract more customers to your detailing business. Marketing is key and it must be consistent. As a growing business owner and operator, this is how I have scaled my business up to over 6 figures and adding multiple streams of income to it.

You don't have to have 7 businesses to be a millionaire, the saying is you need 7 streams of income to reach that status in life. With the business you have, just add other ways you can solve problems with and build that business up.

A letter from Titus

I hope that this book has helped you learn more about entrepreneurship and business. Take this information and execute on it and allow the motivation to push you farther than you have ever went. You owe it to yourself to change the cycle of life you've been repeating.

Today everything changes!

WRITE YOUR END OF THE YEAR GOALS

Read Habakkuk 2:2-3

WRITE YOUR 2024 GOALS

Read Habakkuk 2:2-3

www.ingramcontent.com/pod-product-compliance
Lightning Source LLC
Chambersburg PA
CBHW070522220526
45467CB00002B/798